# Amazon FBA

*(Quick Reference)*

*Getting Amazing Sales Selling*
*Private Label Products on Amazon*

# Table of Contents

# Introduction

The Internet is a realm of endless possibility, especially for businesspeople. It offers an accessible entry into the world of business for all kinds of people with all kinds of budgets. As a modern consumer, you've most likely made at least one purchase online (especially if you're thinking of selling online!). The range of products available online is endless, and growing fast.

Amazon has developed a simple, easy-to-use platform for their own business as well as for sellers looking for an easy way to connect with customers and get their product on the market. Although it began as an online bookstore, it has expanded to offer nearly every product imaginable. The Fulfillment By Amazon (FBA) program allows Amazon and private sellers to help each other--a seller who is willing to do the research and hard work to choose the right product and market it effectively can benefit from Amazon's logistics network, customer care services, and overall reputation. In turn, Amazon charges a small fee for these services as well as for hosting the product listing on its site. In this book, we'll explain how you can build a business using the site, from choosing a product to developing a relationship with your customers and building a long-term strategy for maintaining and growing your business. We'll tell you everything you need to know to identify and understand your target market and to avoid many common mistakes people make when starting out.

The earliest stages of developing a business through Amazon can be some of the most exciting, but it's easy to become overwhelmed by all there is to learn about the process. The little tasks that will help you make sure that your business is profitable and sustainable can seem endless. You can think of this book as your road map through these first weeks, something you can keep by your side to consult when you feel unsure about some aspect of the process, or have questions. We recommend that you familiarize yourself with the whole book before beginning your journey as an FBA seller so you know exactly where you're headed from Day One. As with any business, it's important to have a business plan that you are following from the very beginning. In the following pages, we'll tell you exactly what this means and what you have to do to have your best chance of success as an Amazon seller.

Finally, remember that one of the greatest benefits that comes with starting an independent business is that it allows you to spend your time doing something you're passionate about, and hopefully even earn a living from it!

So get ready, have fun, and good luck!

# Chapter 1: What is 'Fulfillment by Amazon' and What Makes It So Great?

Simply put, 'Fulfillment by Amazon" (FBA) is a way for you to use Amazon's huge, well-developed network of facilities to streamline the process of selling through their website. By sharing responsibilities for each order with Amazon, a new seller can use Amazon's reputation and services to jump-start their own businesses and build a customer base. Many independent online businesses have begun through Amazon FBA, as sellers have used the opportunity of Amazon dealing with many of the day-to-day tasks of running a business to give them the time and resources they need to eventually launch their own website, blog, etc., and become fully independent sellers.

## How It Works

As a third-party seller, your job is to choose a product that you want to sell, then to secure a supplier and develop a marketing strategy. Amazon manages the sales process by hosting your listing and filling the orders you receive with your product, stored at one of their fulfillment centers.

You will arrange for your product to be sent from the supplier you choose to Amazon, which will store it in one of its "fulfillment centers," warehouses spread through many US states to allow for quick delivery and efficient shipping practices. While you handle the ordering process as well as marketing for your product, Amazon will fulfill your orders by shipping your product to whoever orders it. Many FBA sellers continue to work with Amazon long-term, while many others ultimately decide to use the reputation they've built with customers and their honed business savvy to begin to sell through a website or blog that they run themselves.

## Why It Works

FBA also streamlines the shipping process, often a major point of confusion and a potential hassle for those who are new to running their own online business. Even better, Amazon offers two-day Prime shipping on FBA orders as well as free shipping on orders over $35. Short turnaround times allow you to make a positive impression on customers, and that will translate to better reviews and more business. Amazon also provides customer service to your customers. This lets you rest easy in the knowledge that your customers are talking to professionals who know Amazon's practices inside and out.

# Chapter 2: What Are 'Private Label Products'- Why are they Better?

True to its name, Amazon can seem like a jungle to the uninitiated. In this chapter, we'll provide a basic outline of the site's structure from the perspective of a seller. We'll discuss the advantages of selling private label products, and explain why they offer new sellers the best chance to develop a stable, sustainable business.

## Private Label Products vs. Reselling

Amazon sellers fall roughly into two groups--resellers, who buy retail products and resell them on Amazon at a profit, and those who sell products purchased directly from suppliers. The logic behind reselling is simple and often attractive: by offering products that customers want at a higher price than they paid for it, resellers can turn a quick profit. However, there are many downsides to this approach. Although some resellers do make a profit, the fact that they are selling someone else's product means that the opportunities for developing a brand are extremely limited. Because of this, their business effectively ends when their inventory runs out. Reselling also limits your potential to sell within many of the so-called "restricted categories" on Amazon. If your products cannot be listed in the appropriate category, they will be listed in the "Everything Else" category, limiting your sales potential.

## Selling Private Label Products

To start a private label FBA business, you need to be prepared to spend some money before seeing a profit. But this doesn't mean that selling private label products is an option only available to people who have already had success in another business venture. FBA is accessible to most people who are either already supporting themselves or do have a little extra money to work with. You can scale your business and product choices to reflect the amount of time, money, and energy you have.

# Chapter 3: How to Do the Research and Choose a Product

A huge range of products can be sold through FBA, and if you don't have experience in marketing or product development, it's easy to feel like you're already in way over your head. In this chapter, we'll go through a few easy ways to develop an understanding of the kind of products that are in consistent high demand on the FBA market, and we'll outline a few steps you can take to be sure you choose the right product to begin building your business.

## Choosing A Market, Choosing a Product

With the right product, starting an FBA business becomes infinitely easier. The most important question a new seller needs to ask themselves when looking for a product is whether they will be able to build a brand around that product. Amazon is a great resource for people looking to start their own businesses, but a strong brand is the real foundation of a successful business. But the first detail you have to take care of is choosing a marketable product!

The first thing we recommend doing when starting out on the journey of choosing a product is simply writing down with a pen an a piece of paper (or your computer, of course!) and writing a list of things you like to do. The list could include hobbies, family activities, or even just chores and the endless daily tasks that keep life going. Think of the things you use to get these things done. If you use something every day, chances are that there are hundreds of thousands of other people who do too. Any of these items might be a great first product. Or, make a list of everything you touch for

24 hours. With these exercises, you'll gain even more insight into the kinds of items that people need.

Many successful FBA sellers make a habit of watching QVC to get a sense of the products that are available, or even Shark Tank!. You'll develop a much better idea of which products might be of interest of you as you investigate how to grow your business even further.

Also, keep a close eye on eBay and Amazon. Take a little time to look at these sites and make lists of categories, sub-categories, and even specific products that might be of interest to you. Arm yourself with as much information as you can, so you'll be able to make an informed decision!

## Restricted Categories

A number of Amazon categories require an application process and approval from Amazon before a seller can list their products there. A full list of categories and their restrictions can be found here:

http://www.amazon.com/gp/help/customer/display.html?nodeId =14113001

Amazon restricts these categories to reduce the number of short-term, unreliable sellers on the site. The application process typically involves providing receipts from wholesalers with the seller's name on them to prove that the seller is sourcing their goods in a manner that complies with Amazon's standards. Typical reselling practices make this impossible. Some popular categories do not require restrictions, and these may be more practical for a potential seller who is planning on maintaining a fairly small-scale business.

# Narrowing the Field

Once you've thought of a product you might sell, think of five additional products that are closely related to that central item. Take the time to plan ahead a little, so you'll be able to make the most of your own success should you choose that product. Check out the "Frequently Bought Together" section toward the bottom of an Amazon listing. This can lead you in new directions for adding additional products to your brand.

It's important to be aware of Amazon's definition of an "oversized product" and how it affects your product selection process. Your product should way no more than 2 lbs, but 1 lb would be even better for the overall product weight. Similarly, your product should be no more than 18 inches in length. Anything longer is considered an oversize product, and these can be sent in increments of no more than 500 units or less, which puts a considerable limit on your selling potential. Many successful FBA sellers make it a rule not to sell electronics and products with many moving parts, which are likely to break.

# Picking A Winner

After you've narrowed down your list of potential products to about ten contenders, it's time to go back to Amazon and eBay to do a little more research. The first thing you want to look for is whether there is already a well-established presence for the product. For your first product especially, it's best to choose something with proven selling power.

The two most important things to look at when evaluating an established product on Amazon are the BSR, or "best seller rank," and the reviews. The top seller of your prospective product should have a BSR of 500 or less. Check not only the top seller but also down to the sixth-most popular product's BSR. Ideally, the third- and fourth-place products should have roughly a 1500 BSR, and the fifth and sixth about 5000. This shows you that there is demand, but there's also room in the market for you to break in and establish a meaningful presence.

The number of reviews on a product will tell you the most about the product's potential. A top-selling product with more than 500 reviews would not make a good first choice for someone just starting out, but an exception is those products where the next three most popular have well under 500 reviews, or even under 300.

Monitor the sales and ratings of products you're interested in selling over a period of seven days. If you see major changes from one day to the next to the BSR, reviews, or product ranking, this is a good indication that the seller ran a promotion that just began or ended during your period of monitoring.

Finally, take a look at how many products on average a seller is offering. This information will be invaluable in the long run for understanding your possibilities for expanding your own business.

# Chapter 4: Finding A Supplier (Ideally on Alibaba)

Do a quick search at sites such as Alibaba to see what kinds of products are already available to give you an idea of what kinds of products are currently available from wholesalers.

## Choosing A Supplier

The largest and most popular supplier is Alibaba (alibaba.com). Many of the products sold through FBA are sourced through Alibaba, and it's a great choice for sellers just starting out. It allows you to find and connect with a manufacturer, and to order and customize products. Spend some time on the site just looking around to familiarize yourself with the way it works.

You can also use aliexpress.com. On Aliexpress it's easy to buy only one item at a time. Aliexpress does not have the large order minimums of Alibaba, and it also handles shipping. However, it's difficult to customize a product without working closely with the supplier, and many suppliers will be reluctant to put the extra effort and resources into your order for a small order. Some FBA sellers cope with this by buying a relatively small initial order of a product, listing it on Amazon and getting a few initial sales, and then contacting the seller for a larger order of a customized product.

Alibaba uses several search filters. One is "Trade Assurance," on the top right corner of the site's homepage. This offers some compensation should there be something wrong with an order. Another filter will show only "Gold Suppliers." These suppliers pay a yearly fee, and they are subject to on-site checks or other forms of detailed oversight by the site. You can also search only for suppliers who have been subject to an on-site check of their facilities by Alibaba or a third-party company. There is also an option to search "assessed suppliers," which are held to similar standards as those suppliers that have been subject to an on-site check.

Keep in mind that using these filters, especially in combination, may result in fewer search results. You can prioritize for yourself which is most important to you when looking at potential suppliers.

## Communicating with Potential Suppliers

Once you've identified a few different potential suppliers for your product, you can email them through Alibaba. Ask all the questions you might have in the first email to cut down on the inevitable long response times that might slow down the ordering process. It's also a smart move to present your questions as a numbered list. These are the main questions you should ask a potential supplier in your first email (adjusted, of course, for your particular product!):

1. Do you offer samples? How much do samples cost, including shipping? (most sellers use DHL for shipping from suppliers, and you should specify this in your email, along with your ZIP code so they can include exact shipping costs.)

Don't be surprised if the quoted price for samples comes out to somewhere between $30 and $50, even if the samples themselves are free. This is a typical price for express shipping from China to the United States.

2. How long will it take for me to receive the samples?

3. Can I pay using PayPal? (Most experienced FBA sellers will only work with suppliers who accept either PayPal or credit card as forms of payment.)

4. What are the customization options for the product?

5. What is the total cost per unit, including shipping? (Specify the shipping company you are planning on using and the ZIP code to which you plan to have the units shipped.)

6. Do you accept escrow payments? (Alibaba's escrow service provides protections to both buyers and sellers.)

Remember that many oversized products must be shipped by boat. It may be easier for a beginning seller to avoid oversize products until you are more familiar with the ordering process.

Many suppliers will specify the minimum amount of units in an order, often in the thousands. Don't let that discourage you from requesting a smaller sample order from them, especially if you include in your email a note about the possibility of larger orders in the future should you choose to sell the product. A typical request might ask for a test-order of 500, with the possibility of future orders between 1500 and 5000. If a supplier insists on a large initial order, it may not be worth continuing to work with them.

It's not a good idea to describe yourself as an individual trying to get into selling on Amazon. This may give suppliers the impression that you are inexperienced. Instead, introduce yourself as the purchasing agent for your company, along with your full name. This will lend you legitimacy and signal to potential suppliers that you are on equal footing. You can include this information in the first few lines of your email, before you begin asking questions, as well as in your sign off. (The typical sign-off is polite and general, and includes your full name, "Purchasing Manager," and the name of your company).

Finally, draft and email and send it to several potential suppliers at once. This will make it more likely that you will find a good match quickly, and will allow you to compare suppliers in real time.

## Evaluating Potential Suppliers

Ideally, the supplier will provide complete, polite answers to your questions within about twelve hours. A supplier that takes several days to reply, or sends only terse, uninformative answers may prove difficult to work with in the long run. Part of evaluating a specific supplier is, of course, evaluating their product, so it's important to place a small sample order before making your final choice of a product. Once you find a supplier that suits your needs, you'll be communicating back and forth with followup questions until you're ready to place your order. Then, it's time to wait!

# Chapter 5: The Ultimate Guide to Creating A Good Listing that Sells

After you place your order with a supplier, you'll have about 30 days to wait until you receive your product, assuming that you've chosen an overseas supplier. If you happen to have a supplier based in the US, your wait time may be cut in half. Keep this in mind when planning your promotion strategy as much of the work may take place even before you have the product in hand!

## A Great Headline

Use the headline to provide a meaningful introduction to your product for potential customers browsing through search results. Amazon has recently been lowering the maximum number of characters allowed in headlines for listings in various departments (these numbers vary among departments), so take the time to write a headline that uses the space available to you to your best advantage. A good basic rule for a headline is to try to include what the product is and what it does.

## Standout Images

You should provide large, high-definition images of your product, ideally 1500 by 1500 pixels. Have several images available on your listing so the customer can get a good idea of what the product looks like.

Many sellers choose to take the images provided by the supplier to use on their listing. However, this makes it easier for savvy customers and other sellers to trace your product back to the supplier, which can potentially undermine all your hard work on branding and marketing. You can have those images edited a little (or do it yourself), to differentiate them from the source images, but remember that these should be minor changes that don't misrepresent the product.

## A Description that Shines

Your product description should tell anyone viewing the listing everything they need to know to make an informed decision whether or not to buy your product. Be sure to include all of the information you gathered for yourself when deciding to sell the product in the first place, including size, weight, and relevant features.

Many listings use bullet points to make the individual features and advantages of a product even clearer to potential customers. If you use them, shoot for five points total for a complete listing, and be sure to use good grammar in your description.

Finally, at the end of the listing, be sure to mention any warranty or other guarantee you might be offering as clearly as possible. After that, be sure to include a call to action that invites them to click the "Add to Cart" button if they like what they've just read!

# Chapter 6: Launching a Product and Getting Sales Fluidity

Spend the time while you're waiting for your product to ship building interest in your product, and cultivating a base of potential customers through social media marketing and building a "launch list." This way, you'll be getting sales as soon as you're ready to officially launch your product.

## Building Your Launch List

A launch list is simply a list of people with some interest in purchasing your product. Facebook offers a simple, accessible, affordable way to locate potential customers and get some targeted exposure for your product.

First, create a page that relates to your product, without being explicitly devoted to your product itself. For example, if you are selling camping gear, your page should be related to outdoor sports, travel, etc. The goal is to collect "likes" for your page by posting interesting, relevant content 2-3 times a day for your followers to like and share! You can create an ad through Facebook with a simple call to action. You can target an ad only to people who have liked your page, but you can also target it to related pages, so that you can reach people who might be interested in your product. Marketing through Facebook is definitely affordable for most budgets, but it's not free. You should expect to budget $200-$300 for advertising.

While you're assembling your launch list, it's important to think ahead and also assemble an email list which you can use later to expand your promotion efforts. You'll do this by offering a promotion, which we'll cover more in Chapter 7.

## Moving Into the Future

Make sure you have a steady supply of your product as long as your listing is available on the Amazon site. Make a note of how long it took for your product to be shipped from your supplier as well as your sales numbers, and try to estimate when you'll need to restock to make sure that you always have some product available to be shipped to customers.

## Choosing Your Next Product

Once you've established your first product and met your initial sales goals, you might be inspired to start thinking ahead toward when you might introduce a second product (or even a third, or a fourth..). Consider products that can be used with your first product. For example, if you're selling gardening supplies, you might offer a shovel along with a pair of gardening gloves. As you become known for one product you boost your overall sales numbers, and this will be reflected in your profits. The basic rule is, when you're confident that you can sustain a second product as well as your first based on steady sales numbers from your first product, it may be time to consider debuting your next item.

# Chapter 7: Getting a Foothold in your Niche using PPC and Promotions

You will inevitably learn more and more about your place as a seller as you go through the experience of developing your business, and hopefully you'll keep gaining useful insight as you go. Here we'll be discussing strategies for gaining an understanding of your place in the market and your potential for identifying and reaching new customers, and eventually growing your business.

## Pay-Per-Click 101

The basic principle behind Pay-Per-Click (PPC) is simple: in exchange for a higher ranking in search results for a given keyword, you pay a certain amount for each time someone clicks on your listing   PPC can be an effective tool, especially for those just starting out.

It's essential to do your research on the right keyword to use. Be sure to carefully review all potential keywords and the respective search results they generate when making a decision about which one to use PPC for.

Your PPC promotion will be part of your overall marketing strategy. A good starting budget for your PPC marketing would be $10 per day, with $.75 per click. By dedicating a fairly high percentage of your overall budget to each click, you'll make sure that you're high up in the search results for your keyword, making it more likely that each paid click will result in a purchase.

Once you have established yourself a little more on the FBA market and become more familiar with the most common search terms used to find your product, you can expand and diversify your PPC strategy. Adding keywords to your PPC strategy will give you even more sales potential to respond to customer behavior. Once you've established a steady rate of sales (5-10 per day for 5-10 days is a good goal), you can consider expanding.

Competitors' listings are, as ever, a key resource for your evolving marketing strategy. You can use the website amzshark.com to "scrape" your competitors' listings for the keywords most frequently used to reach their products to quickly hone in on the niche you are trying to get into and reach further into your ideal customer base without wasting time, money or energy on unnecessary guesswork.

## Other Promotional Strategies

Start building a foundation for your subsequent products early, even before you have chosen them. You can offer a coupon or promotional code toward the purchase of your second product to the first thirty people (for example) who buy your first product to makes it more likely that these people will return to your listings and become repeat customers.

A great deal of your effort in marketing will be toward the goal of generating word-of-mouth promotions for your product. Maintain a web presence beyond the page on which you're selling itself to understand your products overall reputation. This will also give you a better idea of what customers are looking for. Remember also that customers are also very willing to give word-of-mouth negative reviews! Even if they are harshly worded, your negative reviews may contain valuable insights that can help you strengthen your business.

# Chapter 8: Initial Pricing Strategies (For Launch and Long Term)

The most important factor in ranking keyword search results on Amazon is the sales success of your product. A high ranking exposes your product to more potential customers. This is why many sellers choose to run promotions in the early weeks after launching their product. By getting a lot of sales early, you can get a foothold in your market and working your way up the rankings.

You may have to spend several hundred dollars in product and marketing costs before you begin to see significant sales. It's important to take a balanced approach between short-term profits and long-term potential to succeed. From this perspective, running promotions through your launch list, or even pricing your product lower for everyone in its first few days on the market makes a lot of sense. Don't be afraid, however, to raise your price once you start seeing steady sales rates. As you move up in search results, your selling power will grow by itself.

Keep an eye on your competitors' prices when setting your price. You can use the site camelcamelcamel.com to easily track the pricing history of any product on Amazon. Try plugging in a few of your competitors' listings to the site to see how they have approached pricing in the past, and the way this compares with their current prices. But remember that your pricing decisions should be based on longer-term research and a solid strategy, rather than a momentary urge to undersell the competition. Choose a price that works with your budget and your long-term business goals.

# Further Down the Road: Tax Issues

In order to find out where you are obligated to collect sales tax, you first have to determine where you have so called "sales tax nexuses." This information is available in your seller account on Amazon. To find out where your inventory has been stored, go to Amazon Seller Central, click on "Reports," and from there, go to "Fulfillment." You can use this to generate an "Inventory Event Detail Report." Remember to choose the date you began selling on Amazon as the start date for the report so you can be sure to see every state in which your inventory has been stored for any amount of time.

There will be a "Fulfillment Center" column in the generated report that will tell you every fulfillment center your inventory has been held in. This can be confusing initially, but keep in mind that fulfillment centers are named by the closest airport. Complete lists of airport codes are easy to find on the Internet, and Amazon publishes a complete list of its fulfillment centers with their locations.

After you have assembled a list of states in which your inventory has been stored, you need to apply for sales tax permits in those states. You can do this online through the site of your state's taxing authority. States have different rules about these permits. Some charge an application fee, while others allow you to apply for free. Some require you to renew your permit periodically, while others do not. Once you receive your permit, the state where you registered will give you a "filing frequency," letting you know how often you're required to file taxes in that specific state. Once you have your permit, you can start collecting sales tax (collecting sales tax without a permit is technically unlawful in many states).

Remember that you have to collect sales tax on all transactions in a given state, not only FBA transactions.

Getting your tax status in order isn't fun, but it's worth doing to ensure a sustainable future for your FBA business, and it's something worth considering when you are setting up your initial pricing structure.

# Chapter 9: Boosting Your Seller Ranking and Collecting Feedback

In this chapter, we'll give you a few strategies for moving up in the product rankings and making sure you receive good feedback from your customers!

## Why Is Feedback Important?

In the world of Internet commerce, any guarantee that someone is trustworthy is infinitely more valuable than in real-life situations. This is why feedback that is visible (and positive!) on your sales is one of the greatest assets you'll ever have as a seller. Your potential customers need a reason to trust you, and there's no better indication for them of what they should do than the experiences of those who have bought before them.

## How To Get Started

You can use the social connections you already have to give your customers the assurance they need, by politely asking friends and family if they would be willing to review your product (in exchange for a free sample, of course!). You can ask them if they'd be willing to use your product, think about it, and leave a review in the next 24 hours if they like it.

## Other Ways to Get Feedback

For products sold through FBA as well as any other channel on the Internet, the support of bloggers and others with established reputations who have an established platform for expressing their opinions and a solid audience who trusts what they say is one of the biggest assets a seller can have. If you already follow popular bloggers whose content relates to your product, you can ask them personally to promote your product in much the same way you would a friend or family member in real life.This is a great way to reach a targeted audience with a specific interest in the product you have to offer.

Many sellers also use tomoson.com, a site that connects bloggers and sellers for so-called "Influencer Marketing." As a seller, you can list your product on the site, and people will apply to review it, in exchange for some kind of compensation. Before approving someone to review your product, you can see how much overall influence they have. This might be measured in followers for their blog or twitter or other social media presence.

Be very clear about the terms of the agreement. For example, if you're offering a free sample of the product in exchange for a review, be clear about how shipping is going to work. Taking the time to be sure of the details will help prevent negative feedback from reviewers surprised by extra costs or hurdles in receiving your product.

Use these services with caution. Too much time, energy, and money sunk into generating hype for your product will make it harder for you to earn back what you sink into the effort, and may take your time away from making sure that the sales process is running smoothly. With time and effort, you'll start to generate organic sales, and this will attract further sales. Making sure that you are offering a high-quality product is always the best marketing strategy.

# Chapter 10: Weeding Out Bad Product Reviews (and keeping the good ones)

In this chapter, we'll discuss the different ways you can deal with negative feedback. We'll go over the basic purpose of feedback and the kinds of reviews you should have reviewed by Amazon for potential removal, as well as different ways to encourage positive feedback from satisfied customers.

## What Is Feedback For? (And What Is It Not For?)

The purpose of feedback is to give customers a place to reflect on and review their purchasing experience with you, and to point future buyers in the right direction. If you receive a negative review that focuses on the product itself, remember that you can flag it for review and potential removal by Amazon.

## Encouraging Good Feedback

Customers who buy from Amazon frequently are most likely familiar with the process and may be more likely to leave a review for you, but more casual shoppers may be unfamiliar with the process. If you're communicating with a customer about a detail of the product you can respectfully ask them to leave a review if they have had a positive experience buying from you. It's also a good practice to personally message people who give you good (five-star, four-star) reviews thanking them for doing so.

As your business volume grows, it may become difficult for you to keep communicating with individual customers with the same level of personalization available to you early on in your career as a seller. Fortunately, there are tools available to you to make this aspect of your business easier. Feedback Genius (www.feedbackgenius.com) is a tool that many sellers use to set up automatic communication with their customers. It can help you ask for positive feedback from customers, and it can also let you know as early as possible when you've received negative feedback.

## Paying for Reviews and Other Controversial Practices

Using sites like Tomoson to get product reviews is not a universally respected practice among FBA sellers. Nevertheless, it is fairly common, and if done ethically is a good way to get fair, honest feedback that can help you get ahead in your market. However, some sellers also choose to simply pay for reviews from individuals who have never seen or used the product in question, or even to create alternate accounts themselves to leave glowing reviews that may mislead potential customers.

We would warn you against this as much as possible. The benefits of having positive reviews on your product are less meaningful if they don't reflect as much as possible an organically assembled customer base.

# Chapter 11: Our Top 20 Tips for Amazon FBA Private Label Selling

First of all, choose a product you're passionate about! Building an FBA business is a lot of hard work, but it's infinitely easier if you truly believe in the product you're working so hard to bring to your customers.

Consider also the value of choosing a slightly less popular product. The ideal spot for you to occupy as a new seller is between very well-established products offered by many successful sellers, and unheard of products that have little to no sales presence on the Amazon site. Once you're more established, you'll have the reputation and flexibility to try your hand at selling riskier products.

Many sellers also report success selling bundled products. It's much less likely that another seller will be selling the same group of products as you than when you choose to sell only one product at a time, so you can set yourself apart with this strategy.

Value your position as a small seller. This allows you to develop close relationships with your customers, who will be able to feel that there's a person behind the business, which at the end of the day is a better and more enjoyable interaction than dealing with a faceless corporation focused first of all on their bottom line.

Even though you are a small seller, consider registering as a professional seller. Amazon charges you 15% commission per sale regardless of which type of seller you are, but individual sellers are charged an additional $.99 per sale, while professional sellers pay a flat monthly fee of $39.95. This way, if you sell more than forty units a month, being a professional seller is the most economical choice.

It's easy to get caught up in a "race to the bottom" pricing war with your competitors. But don't let this undercut your profits by letting yourself be drawn into the practice of underselling your competitors. Engaging in pricing wars will only undercut your profits, and take away valuable time that you could use building your business in more lasting ways.

Remember to check your sales rankings and those of your competitors often. These rankings can change dramatically in a short span of time, often several times a day. In order to get an accurate general picture of your place in the market, check your rankings repeatedly over time, and don't forget to keep doing this once you become more established!

Writing a compelling product description that makes potential customers stop and take a closer look as they browse through product listings is a skill, and one that develops and gets easier with time. Make sure that your listing is free of errors not only in its description of your product, but also that it uses good grammar, complete sentences, and correct spelling. Also, if you're using bullet points in your listing, remember to capitalize the first word of every point.

When evaluating competitors' listings, it's also helpful to check to see if the product is listed specifically as FBA. Some products will say that they are fulfilled by "merchant." This is important to note because Amazon has a greater interest in promoting FBA products, as it stands to make a greater profit from these. Keep this in mind when evaluating the influence a particular listing has on your perception of your own presence on the Amazon site.

Many sellers choose to simply copy another seller's listing, with the reasoning that it's likely to bring you as much success as it did the original author of the listing. However, we advise against this. Not only are you missing out on a valuable opportunity to set yourself apart in the eyes of your customers, but you're also taking on all the drawbacks of the listing that might not be immediately apparent to you. We'll bet that you're more than capable of writing an effective listing that will bring in sales, especially since you're doing your research! Don't give up this opportunity to distinguish yourself from your competitors and make a great first impression on your customers!

In the same vein, take the time to communicate with your customers! This can be communicating with them about questions they have regarding your product, well-crafted promotional emails for your product or brand, or just saying thank you for a purchase or a good review! They'll be able to tell that you took the time to make sure they had an enjoyable experience purchasing from you, and that will show in your revenue and your feedback.

Feedback is one more area that can always use more focus. Remember that you do have some control over the reviews that customers see, and that if you receive a negative review, you may have the option of having it removed. Take the time to read your reviews and respond to them if necessary.

As we said earlier, there are many opportunities available on the web to pay for positive feedback. But we recommend strongly that you ignore these in favor of spending your energy on building good relationships with real customers. This will pay off in the long run with repeat business and often surprisingly effective word-of-mouth recommendations.

Amazon offers several tools for FBA sellers to track their sales, and these can be very helpful, especially if you don't have a lot of experience running your own business. However, businesses are as different as the people who run them, and many successful sellers make a point of keeping their own records outside of the Amazon system. This way you'll be able to factor in extras that

Amazon's system doesn't, including the costs associated with securing an inventory, as well as how much of your time you're putting into growing your FBA business. Whether or not you choose to establish a business presence outside of Amazon FBA, keeping your own records allows you to be more in control of every aspect of your business.

It does happen that Amazon will sometimes lose products in their fulfillment centers, and you'll have to contact their seller support services to resolve the problem. The plus side here is while some error is inevitable, Amazon does have a great seller support service in place and your problem will likely be resolved quickly. However, this is another reason to keep your own records--having a complete picture of your business as it is right now in front of you will equip you to catch errors and problems quickly and take the necessary steps to resolve them.

When you create a listing, you register your product's UPC (Universal Product Code) with Amazon. This code is unique to your product and is provided by the supplier. However, it's important to make sure that the seller has not changed your UPC, or has not provided a product with a different UPC. This will help you be sure that your customers are receiving the product you are offering them, and will help you avoid receiving negative feedback.

Remember also that there's no surefire way of predicting what will or will not sell. You can increase your chances of success immensely by learning from other sellers who are successful and thoroughly researching your target market, but it's also possible that even if you do take the time to do this, your product may simply not sell as well as you had hoped, especially in its early days on the market. Our best advice here is to be patient, to continue to work on advertising and product promotions, and to keep looking for new ways to improve your listing! Through the initial learning curve that every seller goes through, it's always possible to learn more and refine your strategy as you gain experience.

It's tempting to ignore tax issues in favor of growing your business in other areas. But we can't stress enough how important it is to take your tax status seriously, especially if you have long-term plans for your business beyond small-scale selling on FBA. If you don't file taxes, it might take years for anyone to notice, but once they do, you'll be required to pay all taxes out-of-pocket, as well as penalties and interest whether or not you have been collecting sales tax on individual transactions.

As you continue selling on Amazon, you'll almost certainly come up with more questions. While we've done everything possible to provide you with a great foundation for your FBA venture, it may help you to consult more people who are going through the challenges and triumphs of the life of an FBA seller along with you. Consider seeking out message boards and online communities of sellers, or check out one of the many popular websites or podcasts run by sellers with a proven track record of success. As you gain knowledge and experience, you may also be able to serve as an example for other sellers who are just starting out!

Keep in mind that Amazon has an app, Amazon Seller, that many FBA sellers use to keep up with their business on the go. This can be an extremely helpful tool to keep track of your business on the go!

# Conclusion

Thank you again for downloading this book!

We hope you've found everything you wanted to know about FBA selling on Amazon! We've taken you through every step of the process, from understanding more about how FBA works, to choosing a product, through to building your business into a long-term source of income!

If you've finished this book, you now know everything you need to know to get started as an FBA seller with a working knowledge of the tools available to you to streamline your process and grow your business. But this book is organized for easy reference, so you can always refer back to a chapter if you need to refresh your memory. We hope we can help you throughout your journey as an FBA seller!

We've talked a lot in this book about the importance of customer feedback. And now it's time to very literally take a page from our own book and ask you to leave us some feedback on the book's Amazon listing! If you liked the book, don't be afraid to speak up and let us know! We really appreciate the honest opinion of each and every one of our satisfied customers.

Thank you one last time, and good luck!

www.ingramcontent.com/pod-product-compliance
Lightning Source LLC
Chambersburg PA
CBHW070747180526
45168CB00004B/1557